CW00767060

Flat and Boring
There Isn't It?

A celebration of life in the Lincolnshire Fens

This Book is dedicated to the person who, in 2008, forced us into bankruptcy and made us sell our house.

Thank you.
Best thing anyone ever did for us!

Flat and Boring There Isn't It?

A celebration of life in the Lincolnshire Fens

Amanda Pearson

PAUL DICKSON BOOKS

Flat and Boring There Isn't It?

A celebration of life in the Lincolnshire Fens

Published by Paul Dickson Books, April 2023
Paul Dickson Books, 156 Southwell Road, Norwich NR1 3RP,
t. 01603 666011,
e. paul@pauldicksonbooks.co.uk, www.pauldicksonbooks.co.uk

© Amanda Pearson, 2023

All rights reserved. No part of this publication may be
reproduced or transmitted in any form or by any means,
electronic or mechanical, including photocopying, recording,
or any information retrieval or storage system, without permission
in writing from the publisher.

Amanda Pearson has asserted the moral right to be identified as
the author of this work.

ISBN 978-1-7397154-2-7

A CIP catologue record for this book is available from the
British Library

Designed by Brendan Rallison
Photograph of author: Steve Duncan
Printed in Norwich by Interprint

CONTENTS

Synopsis – What's this all about then?

You may think the title of this book is slightly odd, so let me explain its origin, and the reason I chose it to grace the cover of this collection of poems and prose, plus the reason this book exists at all.

I was born and raised in the Fenland area of South Lincolnshire, not far from the most Westerly corner of the square "bite" out of the East coast that is The Wash. I always enjoyed the relative quiet of my small, market, hometown and would defend it against anyone who dared criticise. And although that town has expanded and changed a huge amount, I believe my husband and I would still be living in our edge of town, 1970's four-bed detached, for which we had wonderful plans for expansion and improvement, had fate not taken a hand. In 2008 "circumstances beyond our control", which in actual fact was bankruptcy forced on us when my husband's largest client went into liquidation with thousands in unpaid bills, saw us forced to sell the town house, and move to a rental in what a friend once described as "just beyond the back of beyond". The new home was a bit of a last-resort choice, after failing to find anything either suitable or affordable to rent in the town we were used to, we took a risk on the countryside. Now, after over 13 years in our "temporary new home" we are struggling to think about ever moving away. Living in the truly rural heart of the Fenlands has given me an even deeper appreciation of the area we call home.

Our landscape is much maligned and sadly underrated, with most people seemingly assuming that a flat landscape must be boring, why would you even want to visit, let alone live there? The "flat and boring" description is one quoted all too often by people who have never even visited. These people soon realise they have "hit a nerve" when I begin to extol, at length, the virtues of landscapes with views that end only at the horizon, and dramatic skyscapes, sunrises and sunsets. As I am quick to argue, few would refuse a sea view, and there is not much by way of hills to look at when you gaze out to sea.

I love being creative, sewing, cooking, photography, and also writing. I often write lengthy e-mails to my American-born but half-English cousin, who enthusiastically soaks up any and every detail I feed her about her late mother's homeland. One day, during a video call discussion with a group of friends musing on possible alternative careers for some of us, my cousin suggested maybe I should write, as she really thought others would be interested in reading the kind of thing I sent her, descriptions of our life in the flatlands, the surroundings, the nature, and our transition from town to country dwellers. That spark of suggestion caught on the many scraps of creative kindling littering my brain, and soon I was burning up pages with prose about our life in rural Lincolnshire. However, on reading back through the resulting pile of ramblings, I was not at all convinced that anyone would have the patience to plough through the spilled contents of my overcrowded mind, never mind paying for the privilege to do so. I decided the work needed structure and rhythm to make it manageable. I had dabbled in poetry years ago, albeit comic poetry at work, it seemed to strike a chord with people, so I set about converting the chaotic prose to rhyme. I combed out the tangle of words and gave them form, the discipline forcing me to choose words carefully to express accurately what I wanted to portray, I then set the scene for each poem with a shorter section of prose. I sent a few of the resulting poems to family and friends, who seemed to enjoy them, though of course there is always the danger they are simply being kind. Over the course of around a year I managed to form the tangled prose, plus a pile of new verses that kept popping up in my head, into a reasonable semblance of a book of poetry people may actually want to read.

Another year of editing later, and I now invite you to join me for a walk, a lovely easy walk as there are no hills, through the landscape that has become part of who I am. I will endeavour to prove to you that The Fens, while undeniably flat, are anything but boring.

Amanda Pearson
South Lincolnshire Fens
February 2023

A
Different
Life

New sights, sounds and experiences, we become country mice

Bringing Out the Inner Country Mouse

Most people have heard of, if never read, the tale of the town mouse and the country mouse, about two friends trying out and learning to appreciate each other's very different lifestyles.

I grew up within walking distance of the centre of a market town, my husband grew up in a village, but it was a large, well serviced one, and he lived on a housing estate, so our surroundings were not so very different. When we married, we lived first in a large village, then later back in town where we brought up our children. For the two of us in our mid-forties, plus our teenage son who had not yet flown the nest, the move to a house in the middle of farmland, with no near neighbours, came as a bit of a culture shock.

I often use the phrase "born again" to describe people who newly take to something with way more enthusiasm than anyone who has been doing that same thing all their life, like the businessman who, in the throes of a mid-life crisis, buys a huge, expensive motorbike and shiny new racing leathers – born-again biker.

So when I look at myself, born and bred "townie", now enthusiastically fighting vicious brambles to pick blackberries, tackling a brace of pheasants left hanging outside our back door to prepare them for the pot, or wielding an axe to split kindling, I have to confess – I am a born-again country mouse.

We'd never been country mice, we lived in the town,
until fate took a hand and turned life upside down.

We sold up our old life to pay off our debts,
took a deep breath, and decided to face
a new challenge, a change is as good as a rest,
we decided we'd put country life to the test.

Moved out from warm, seventies' cavity walls,
to crumbling red brick almost two centuries old.
Away from the neighbours, and traffic all round,
to fields and horizons, and hardly a sound.

From well-maintained tarmac, white lines on the roads,
to tracks with huge potholes, and cracks where grass grows.
From sky that glows orange with streetlight pollution,
to black-velvet evenings when you can't see a thing.

The sounds of the morning, once people and cars,
now the sounds we wake up to are cows, sheep and crows.
We'd turn on the gas to light our lounge fire,
now it's kindling and logs from the woodpile outside.

We've faced new life challenges, risen to them all,
from birds down the chimneys to damp-sodden walls.
A culture shock, yes, but we have no regrets,
never lost the important things, family and friends.

We've been on a learning curve long, fast and steep,
but embraced every moment since we made our leap.
The new life has grown on us, we don't wish to return
to the noise and the chaos of living in town.

We'd thought we were town mice but, deep down inside us,
there were two inner country mice waiting to surface.

Where We Call Home

The Fens are scattered with old farmhouses and farmworkers' cottages. The latter are usually small pairs of semis, many from the early part of the 20th Century. They were originally owned by the farmers whose land they sit on and lived in by farm labourers and their families, the accommodation being part of the workers' wages. Many of these workers' cottages have been sold off, or are now rented out privately, providing a secondary income for the farmers who own them.

The farmhouses are bigger, detached, usually red brick sometimes yellow, they pre-date most of the cottages, being Georgian or Victorian. Some are slightly larger than others, but all remarkably similar in design. Their sheer age means that they come with a plethora of maintenance issues, and some have fallen derelict and been demolished over the years, though there are still many, many left. The ones still standing are continuing to provide welcoming family homes, some still lived in by the farmers who own them, and others like the one we live in are rented out by their owners who have chosen to live elsewhere, or who have bought up a neighbouring farm with a house, so do not need the house themselves. These buildings and their surrounding barns are as much a part of the landscape as the drainage dykes and wheat fields.

Red brick farmhouse.
Like a small child's painting.
Rectangle
with chimneys,
door in the middle.
Symmetrical windows,
like eyes
with fans of red brick lashes.
Eyeliner below
of white painted stone.
Stands in green lawns,
edged by tall beech hedges.
Gravel drive crunches when someone approaches.
For almost two centuries it's gazed over fenland,
kept families safe and warm inside.
Familiar landmarks on Lincolnshire landscape,
all similar, like siblings,
but no two quite the same.
Like so many others,
its sisters and brothers,
it weathers and ages,
but still stands strong and proud.
These houses are special,
they've survived tests of time,
and this one is more-so,
it's where we call home.

Log Fire Season

I grew up in a 1960's bungalow, with a gas fire in the lounge, only ever experiencing a proper blaze at Christmas, when we visited my favourite aunt and uncle, who had a coal fire. Until we moved to our current home I had never lived with a real fire, other than the odd wood-burner in a holiday cottage.

Now we have open fires in our lounge and dining room. The latter is rarely used, as once the room is full of people it hardly needs heat, but the lounge one is used a lot, especially at the changeover of seasons, when it's not cold enough to have central heating on, but still chilly when just two of us sit in the lounge in the evenings.

My husband's line of work is property maintenance, which occasionally involves chopping down trees for people. We are lucky enough to have some old stables as outbuildings, and once a year my husband and his best friend have a log chopping day, cutting up all that has gathered over the year, and stacking it in the stables to dry ready for burning the following year. Myself and friend's wife, who is my best friend, disappear off for some retail therapy while the men "play" with chainsaws and log splitters, our friend takes home a boot full of last year's logs for his efforts.

I soon learned to light a log fire, it still feels more of a novelty than a chore. This is helped by the fact that there is a large bucket sunk in the floor under the fire, called a Baxi grate, meaning that I only need to clean out ash once a week, rather than every day.

Basking in the warm orange glow of flickering flames still feels like a decadent indulgence.

Chilly evening threatens frost.
Safe indoors,
we stack the grate.
Newspaper sheets.
Yesterday's hot gossip
crumpled to ignite today's fire.
Kindling, split from scrap.
Busy hours spent in barns
with saw and axe.
Topped with logs,
cut from trees long felled by chainsaw's razor teeth.
Split to wedges by machine and man.
Now dry
from months and years stacked high
in piles, under cover outside.
Long match lit,
flares orange.
A touch lights paper, soon consumed by hungry flames.
Kindling catches,
burns hotter,
heats wood and bark to orange glow,
which bursts to flickering flame.
Flames grow and spread,
our senses all treated.
Fire crackles and pops, roars gently, the sound of warmth.
Wood burns,
Log fire aroma permeates the room,
reminding us of winter flavours.
Bonfire-baked potatoes, smoky peated whisky.
Flames dance to entertain us
in their finery, bright hues.
Orange and yellow,
highlights of purple and blue.
The room warms,
atmosphere changes,
becoming Christmas card tableau.
Black night windows reflect orange glow.
Whisky glasses and sofas beckon.

The Reluctant Forager

I love food, my waist line will bear testimony to that. Since moving out of town we've become more and more aware of the importance of fresh and local when it comes to food. There is, however, another category I have come to appreciate – Free.

From the abundance of berries in the hedgerows of late Summer or windfall apples from a neighbour, to the odd brace of pheasants I find hanging from the bell outside our back door when there has been a shoot nearby, I try hard to make use of them all.

However, when it comes to foraging, I do have to admit to being extremely risk averse. I'm no Hugh Double-Barrell, venturing into the countryside with foraging friends, plundering nature's bounty. I wish I could confidently stride out and collect chanterelles and burdock root, but I have a deep-seated fear of ending up with toadstools and hemlock, so I do tend to stick to what I am confident I can identify.

At time of writing, all our friends and family have survived my countryside culinary efforts.

Blackberries, ripe, fiercely guarded by brambles,
against the appetites of humans and animals.
The fight with the undergrowth may be bloody and vicious,
but so worth the effort, the results are delicious.

Elderberry heads like black-beaded flowers,
picking them, fingers stained purple for hours.
Rich with vitamins, cold cures they make,
to fend off the germs during cold winter days.

Cherry plums ripen, quick have you heard,
better move fast, or lose all to the birds.
These red and gold jewels are juicy and sweet,
when topped with rich crumble, make the perfect treat.

The blackthorn hides treasure behind long sharp thorns,
black sloes to flavour our favourite gins.
So tough and bitter, it's hard to believe,
mixed with some alcohol, what delights they achieve.

So much food out there, I wish I were braver.
If only I had the courage to savour
a dandelion, nettle, mushroom or rosehip,
walnuts and rowans, all there to be picked.

But confidence fails me as I check in my books,
is that mushroom edible? Best take a look.
Cannot be sure, is the picture the same?
I don't want to take something poisonous home.

One day, I keep saying, I'll take risks and be brave,
but for now, pick the favourites, stay nice and safe.

Trouble With Wind

The title of this piece will perhaps elicit a few giggles from those who, like me, grew up with the gentle humour of Carry On films. However, the wind I refer to here is of the meteorological , rather than the biological, variety. It has nothing at all to do with the over-consumption of any of the many varieties of leafy green vegetable grown locally.

We are all aware that the UK is increasingly troubled by storms and high winds, though here toward the East coast we are lucky in that much of the roughest weather approaches from the West, and has often blown the worst of itself out by the time it gets to us, we just get the heavy sobs at the end of the tantrum. It is not so much this type of wind that bothers us, it's the almost constant strong breeze that blows across the Fens, not powerful enough to do damage, but certainly strong enough to be extremely irritating. You see our wide-open spaces mean that there is absolutely nothing to stop the strong breeze in its tracks. Dustbin lids need a brick on top to prevent them flying off. Washing, should you dare to peg it out, requires good strong pegs to stop it ending up in the next village, and recycling bags need a good weight of glass in them to stop them blowing into the dyke before the refuse collection men pick them up – that's my excuse for the wine bottles anyway.

We deal with these minor irritations day to day, we put up with them. However, the one time the wind really does test my patience is when we try to entertain outdoors. A beautifully set alfresco dining table is somewhat marred by the addition of pegs to hold the tablecloth on and rocks to weigh down the napkins. So even on the most beautiful day, we mostly entertain in the confines of a gazebo with curtains, to prevent salad leaves making a bid for freedom, or the unthinkable - the wind knocking over the wine glasses.

Its' windy.
Again.
It's a problem out here.
The wind will be blowing no mind what time of year.
Icy blasts in the Winter, from the chilly East coast
however, are not what annoys us the most.

The "brisk" Summer breezes are more of a pain,
worse than baking hot sun, or showers of rain.
We can shade from the sun, or the rain, with umbrellas,
but try planning a barbecue, see what it does.

As soon as the very first table is laid,
a soft gentle breeze transforms into a gale.
With nothing to stop it across our flat land,
the wind will wreak havoc, blustering around.

Glasses fall over, and napkins are blown,
along with the tablecloth, away 'cross the lawn.
Umbrellas and parasols turn inside out,
a windbreak erected, by wind is torn down.

We decide to take cover, get the canopy out,
we know the assembly will be quite a fight.
Wrestle cover over frame, get it pulled tight,
it would not be the first one the weather has wrecked.

Guy ropes and tent pegs aplenty employed,
we're determined our picnic will still be enjoyed.
Canopy walls flap in and out, breathing
like huge bellows powered by relentless wind blowing.

We set up our tables, we will not give in,
stoke up the fire-pit, outdoors we will dine.
We're not to be beaten by troublesome weather.
We're British.
Coats on.
We'll eat out whatever.

Bunnies

Whilst you can often walk for miles in this area and hardly see another soul, there are still often ugly reminders of the passing of fellow humans along the way, not to mention their canine companions. This poem voices my irritation at those dog owners who diligently "clear up" after their four- legged friends, but then leave the resulting colourful plastic parcels of pooh dropped in verges, or worse, hung in trees, with their little tie-handle "ears" sticking up.

Pooh-bag bunnies,

    suspended in trees,

and sitting in grass

    where dog walkers have been.

Folks clean up the mess

    their canines have made.

"We follow the law"

    you will hear them say.

But pooh-bags they pile up,

    day after day,

where walkers scoop poop,

    but don't take it away.

The Unfairness of It

While I am of the opinion that those careless dog walkers should be whipped soundly with their own dog leads, I do have a degree of sympathy for those who do clear up as they should. As with so much of life, there is a huge injustice when it comes to clearing up after animals.

A dog walker stoops, trusty pooh bag in hand,

to clear up the mess left behind by their hound.

But it seems when a horse has a pooh, no one minds,

riders don't scoop what their mounts leave behind.

The tail is raised, and down to the ground

falls a steaming great pile in which you could drown.

But the horse can trot on, rider paying no care,

To the serious slip-hazard left behind there.

Out at Nightfall

Streetlights are few and far between in our part of the world, the odd one here and there at a junction, but generally the backroads of the villages are plunged into thick darkness at nightfall. That is unless cloud cover clears, and we have a bright full moon. From inside, our windows on an overcast night are reflective black rectangles. There is no sign of the world outside, we can't even see the hedges just across the lawn, it's like looking at mirror glass. But with a full moon, you can look out in the early hours of the morning, and the world is completely illuminated by moonlight, looking like a black and white photo of its daytime self. It can be lighter at 3am than it is by 6, when the moon has sunk, but the sun not yet emerged from the horizon. Being out on a moonlit night can make you feel as if you are in some kind of alternative reality, all the usual things are there, but nothing looks quite the same. The effect can be beautiful, though at the same time a little unnerving.

I stand at the bridge as the air round me chills.
Twilight is falling over hedgerows and fields.
The sun sinks through clear sky of this late Summer's day,
to a soft bed of cloud, low and pale grey,
which smothers all chance of a glowing red sky.

Colour's sucked from the landscape.
Bright hues drain away,
borrowed to illuminate another place.
The sky is left empty, colourless.

The landscape, trees, hedges, barns, houses, shades of grey,
slowly darken, 'til black silhouettes against the late evening sky.
The odd speck of light in the distance,
bright beacons against the thickening darkness,
a lonely streetlamp, a farmyard light.

A bright full moon, a giant balloon, floats up from the eastern
horizon, Shrinking with distance as it climbs higher, light intensifying.
Illuminating the night world.
Grey tinted surroundings turn sepia,
like faded old photographs, faint hints of colour,
picked out by the glow of our rocky satellite.

Bright silver ribbons sit in dykes dug for drainage,
cutting parallel lines with the roads, disappearing under bridges.
Light from the milk-white orb in the sky picking out still water,
turning daytime dull brown to platinum highlight.

A pale shape glides by, a barn owl in flight.
Searching for prey, flying low over dykes.
A silent white ghost.

Eyes struggle to adjust to the fading night light
changing perception of familiar shapes, painted black, shadows cast
by moonlight.
Is that a hunched figure by the roadside, head down, black cloak,
looming menace?
Is that an arm reaching out from the tree to grab my hair as I pass,
brush my face?

I turn to head home, ready for supper,
the warmth and the glow of a roaring log fire.
I set foot on the drive, gravel crunching underfoot,
a dark fumble with keys and my sanctuary's unlocked.

From the comfort of home I survey
the silver painted world, through the window.
No strange shadows now,
just hedges and trees, barns and houses,
bright edged by the moonlight.
No threat in sight, settle in for the night.

For your entertainment today ....

*Those not "in the know" may dare to label country life "boring".
However, while it may not have bright lights and nightlife, there
is plenty out here to see. The land is always busy with farming
activity, and wildlife just going about its everyday business is always
fascinating, hence the popularity of shows like Countryfile, and so
many nature programmes on TV. Then added to the everyday,
there can be drama and even comedy.*

County life may be quiet, but it's never dull,
each day with activity always full.
It's a wonderful place for relaxation,
but if you care to look, there's also entertainment.

Birds, animals, humans all live in close quarters
and create entertainment to rival soap operas.
There's drama aplenty when species disagree,
about who owns a territory, or where they should be.

Rapid shrieks "caw! caw! caw!" from dense cover of spinney,
is black and white magpie angrily swearing.
The brunt of this bird's vocalised ire?
Black cat stalks below, posing a danger.

A small flock of ewes in the neighbouring paddock,
peacefully munching their grassy breakfast,
spot a wily red fox, daring to venture
into their field, out on an adventure.

Adventure indeed, sheep's hive-mind kicks in,
in a neat pincer-movement they close in on him.
Sensible fox beats a hasty retreat,
doesn't want to be trampled by ovine feet

In a field on his own is a lonely grey donkey,
two sheep are moved in, so he has some company.
But he is not keen on this woolly invasion,
and quickly takes steps to try and evict them.
He chases them round until tired, they lie down,
but he's not having that, he stomps angrily round.

He kicks and he stamps on them, grabs mouths-full of wool,
he wants them to move, he's trying to pull
them up to their feet so they run away,
but they've had enough, sheep don't want to play.
Farmer must part them like arguing children,
antisocial donkey is once more alone.

Many times, like in films, we'll see a road chase,
when some fenced in animal tries to escape.
A lamb will squeeze nimbly through the rungs of a gate.
The donkey slips harness and trots up the road.
A calf bids for freedom, tries jumping wire fencing,
but doesn't quite make it, halfway over he dangles.

A small flock of sheep being herded along,
decide on a wander before they head home.
Many times farmer is called on the phone,
to round up his charges, and take them back home.

Sometimes a drama is real life or death.
See a plummeting sparrow hawk, hold your breath,
as a goldfinch, alerted, darts swiftly for cover
In shrubbery dense, where hawk cannot follow.
The sparrow hawk, thwarted, pulls on the brakes
avoiding collision, back to open air takes.

For light relief, humans will entertain too.
From our upstairs window we had a good view,
of the paddock when farmers arrived to collect cows,
to take them to where they could munch fresh new grass.
Trailer door opens, auburn ladies trot in,
all except, that is, for a troublesome one.

She's no desire to squash in with the others,
she's off down the field, she has other ideas.
The farmers give chase, arms flung open wide.
Like grown men playing aeroplanes, they run round the field.

So you see, living here, there's ne'er a dull moment.
Who needs bars and theatres with so much entertainment.

In Fear of the Drain

The land we live on was claimed from the sea by man many years ago to provide fertile soil for crops. To prevent it from reverting to wetlands and saltmarsh it is criss-crossed by a network of man-made dykes and drains, which divide the fields like drystone walls do in Yorkshire. The dykes feed water, which runs from the fields, to the larger drains, which eventually empty into rivers or the sea.

Much of the main route into our village follows the course of one of the larger drains, with just a narrow verge between the edge of the road and a steep grassy slope of something like 15 feet, which ends at the watery, muddy, bottom of a 30 foot wide trench. Big as they are, the usual water level in the main drains is often only around a foot, the rest of the capacity being available in case of flooding.

Despite the fact that you would have to be extremely unlucky to manage to drown in so little water, much to our amusement, many of the people we know, especially the "sensible" older generation are terrified to drive along by the drain, and will go to almost any lengths to avoid doing it. I myself am much more concerned on a motorway, where you are at the mercy of idiots who manoeuvre erratically, at great speed, with no consideration for others.

All you have to do to reach our house safely is stay on the road – pretty simple really.

Many who visit us travel in fear,
they're afraid of a monster that's lurking out here.
For following the road that leads to our home,
is a terrifying, monstrous, scary drain!

So frightened are they, they'll take huge diversions,
travel miles to avoid, so great's their aversion
to driving next to a field drainage system.
Try to tell them no danger, but they just will not listen.

They're not scared to travel on motorways fast,
don't worry about the speed of oncoming cars.
But ask them to drive where they'll scarce see a soul,
you'd think they'd to travel the road to Hell.

The drain has been there for hundreds of years,
seen traffic change from horses to cars.
I've never heard tell that it reached up and grabbed
a cart or a car, and pulled it down deep.

Just pay good attention, look where you're going,
carelessness anywhere could be your undoing.
Keep control of the steering wheel, stay on the road,
and out from the water you'll not need to be towed.

So come on, man-up people,
I ask once again –
Who's afraid of the Big Bad Drain?

Mud on the Road

To most, the word harvest conjures up visions of combines shaving fields of swaying golden wheat down to stubble, spitting seed into tractors and leaving piles of straw to be gathered and baled. However there are more harvests in the Fens. In the Autumn, fields of fat brassicas lose their heads to rows of migrant workers with cauli knives, and sugar beet and potatoes are lifted from the ground by red-painted, mechanical harvesters. All this produce is loaded on the fields into trucks and tractor trailers. The result of all these harvests is the same, countless heavily laden vehicles, with clay soil made wet by Autumn rain embedded in the thick treads of their tyres, pulling out onto the narrow public roads between the fields.

Consequently, travel on our rural roads in Autumn can become, shall we say, interesting, if you do not respect the conditions.

Roads are slick,
thick
with mud from the fields.

Soon ridges and ruts,
as passing tyres cut
through the grey clods
that cover the roads.

Taking their time,
cutting parallel lines
to be followed, compacted
by traffic behind.

Rain falls,
mud spreads.
Slippery beds
of brown lay where roads were.

Drivers take care.
        Beware.
           It's like ice,
      in a trice
    one false move
  and you'll lose
      control.
        Dykes beckon.

Signs warn,
but still some
think they know better,
can still go faster
than the rest.

Soon victims of their own conceit,
in sugar beet season a common sight,
a break down truck, with pulleys and chains,
hauling the "clever" ones out of the drains.

Commute in the Snow

Before we moved to our current home, I had little experience of driving in bad weather conditions, having mostly lived and worked in town, where roads were well gritted at first sign of frost or snow. The thought did briefly cross my mind that bad weather may affect travel, but we had so rarely seen snow over the last 20 years or so, the thought was only fleeting.

We moved into our new home mid-November, and the following February the weather decided to test this inexperienced driver with the worst snowfall we'd seen in years. However, I was determined not to be beaten, so gave it my best shot to try to cover the 13 miles to work, but had to admit defeat in the end. That was the only time I failed to manage the journey either way, despite being tested again on a couple of occasions, one of which was a journey home from work in 2013, which I describe at the beginning of this poem, using artistic licence to juggle the timeline of events.

The view from work's window says it's snowing tonight,
against 4pm blackness, fat flakes of white,
fall from the sky, landing on pavements,
where white turns to sludge with the passing of footsteps.
I walk to the car park, I climb in my car,
town's lit, snow's still falling, but the roads are all clear.

But my journey is long,
snowfall getting stronger.
Street lighting ends,
and I'm out in the Fens.

Snowflakes, like a screen saver, rush at my windshield,
wind chasing them faster and faster 'cross white fields.
The effect is hypnotic, a moving black tunnel,
lined with bright dots, fast toward me they funnel.

Straining my eyes to see edges of roads,
as slowly by snowfall, with verges they're blurred.
Vehicles approaching across the road,
fat flakes, in the headlight beams explode
into blinding stars and brilliant white light,
reducing to nothing, my field of sight.
Black evening is dense, and wind howling strong,
just ten miles an hour, I'm crawling along.

But a blessing disguised, wind blows snow from my route,
as it howls across fields, drifting snowfall in heaps.
It fills up the dykes with soft white marshmallow,
and piles pure white drifts against buildings and hedgerows.

Further and further, I venture along,
through thick heavy snowfall and East wind so strong.
Finally, safe back at home, wind dies down,
hardly see traffic passing, we're a long way from town.
The snow keeps on falling, but now it's straight down.
the view from our window, thick white duvet all round.

Next morning I wake to a beautiful day,
but yesterday's snowfall is blocking my way.
We're not used to this weather, my car's ill-equipped
to stray onto snowfall, frozen, compact.

My husband and son early on made their way,
I don't want to be beaten, I'll go out today.
But more snow has fallen since they ventured out,
their tracks have been back-filled with powdery white.
My car skids and skitters, like Bambi on ice,
you'd think it was fitted with ice skates, not tyres.
My steering wheel is making mere suggestions,
my car wants to go in its own direction.

Wheels crunch, and creak loudly, compacting the snow.
Three miles I have crawled now, twelve more to go.
Road traffic announcements assail my ears,
warning "don't' risk the journey", listen to your fears.
Knuckles white and nerves shattered I finally give in.
Find the mouth of a junction where gently I turn.
Now facing home, slowly, slowly I creep,
snow's falling again now, settling deep.
I can just see the tracks my car made heading out,
almost covered already, right decision no doubt.
They're filling so quickly, I made the right choice,
to listen to radio's cautionary voice.

Finally, home, I pull on the drive,
amazed and grateful I've safely arrived.
I'll venture no more, car slipping and sliding,
I'll take the day off, and go into hiding.

A Wet Commute

After several months of converting rambling prose to poetry and feeling the rhymes flow easily and freely, to the extent where I found myself on many occasions actually forming descriptions of things in my head automatically in rhyme, I hit a bit of a writer's block. New inspiration did not seem to readily present itself, and I ceased to be able to think in rhyme at all. This was, in actual fact, an almost pleasant respite, as the frustration of having words and verses spin constantly in my head when driving or walking around, with nowhere to be able to commit them to paper, could be surprisingly intense and distracting. The respite was, however, short lived. As I sprinted to my car one morning in the middle of a torrential downpour of rain, the lyrical prose began once again to invade my consciousness, forming quickly into a poetic description of my wet start to the morning.

It's pouring.
Non-stop rain.
From fat drops that fall
from a ripple of gunmetal cloud, pregnant with more,
and splatter like water balloons on roads and roofs,
to fine drifting drizzle
from dove grey sky,
thick in the air,
not falling but wet.
Misting the distant view.

Puddles form
in sunken dips at road edges.
Creeping, like tide,
across tarmac from each side,
to meet in the middle.
Vehicles splash through,
spray like log flumes,
don't be a pedestrian passing by.
Soil darkens to black in the fields.
New shoots, vibrant green,
highlighted bright, despite the gloom

Few birds fly.
Tiny ones hide
in hedgerows
Ducks, swans and moorhens abound.
Their waterproof backs
impervious to the weather driving others to cover.

The calm surface of water,
sitting in drains,
is rippled by precipitation.
Constant.
Raising levels already raised
by rainfall drained from sodden fields.

Wipers work busily to clear
my windscreen, fogged by the rain
which beats constant percussion on steel car roof.
A lorry passing the other way,
huge tyres raising spray
of water and mud,
sends wipers into overdrive,
flapping wildly 'til view is cleared.

Journey over at last.
stop the car,
cast an eye to the sky.
Still it rains.

Hood pulled up,
step out.
Lock car,
head down,
and run for dry land.

Suffering For My Art

The problems of an over-active imagination.

I'm a Verse-oholic

As mentioned previously, after but a short while of converting prose to poetry, I actually began to find it difficult at times not to think in rhyming couplets. The following was my "cry for help"

My brain's crammed with poems, I fear it may pop.
I wrote verse for amusement, now I simply can't stop.
The rhymes keep on flowing, emerge thick and fast,
next jostling for space as I scribble the last.

Like any addiction, it started as fun,
never imagined how hooked I'd become,
Can't look at a sunset, bright orange and red,
without rhyming couplets crowding my head.

I just can't resist it, I'm out of control,
my brain cells bombarded, my mind's in a whirl.
As I try to explain the affliction that haunts me,
my cry for assistance emerges as poetry!

Oriental Adventure

In an attempt to stem the flow of verse invading my every waking moment, I decided to try a new discipline. I had heard of haiku, a Japanese form of poetry which has formal structure, but does not rely on rhyme for its flow. After a short search on the internet, I discovered that a haiku verse consists of 17 syllables, written as three lines, five syllables in the first line, seven in the second and five in the third.

As one prone to ramble, I had my doubts as to whether I could work within such tight parameters, but I do like a challenge, so I started to experiment. To my great surprise I actually found the structure helpful, it focuses the mind wonderfully. With such a limited amount of syllables available you certainly have to prune back and decide which ones to use for maximum effect to describe the subject matter.

I thoroughly enjoyed my venture into the Orient, and some of my efforts are shown on the next couple of pages, and also dotted trough the remainder of this book.

As much as I loved trying out the new discipline, there is one slight problem - I fear I may be addicted!

Mind once full of verse

Invasive rhyming couplets

Haiku swept them out

Haiku - Birdlife

Downy brown Ducklings
In lines run fast to catch Mum
Heading for water

Black and white long-tails
Flit like flying lollypops
Wings too fast to see

Pigeons peck new shoots
Fly up when bird scarer bangs
Vermin of the sky

Sleek black moorhen struts
Bright yellow legs stride head nods
In time to its steps

Pert cheeky robin
Breast glowing red perched on
post
Festive bird watching

Hunting kestrel hangs
Like feathered crucifix still
In the air waiting

Buzzard swoops and squeals
In Summer sky rides thermals
Dark shadow on blue

Mallards loud quacking
Gather round children with bread
Drab hens and bright drakes

Egret glows pure white
Catching sunlight on green bank
Startled quick takes flight

White swan beautiful
Rests peacefully head under wing
On green riverbank

Pheasant waits by road
Bright in colour not in mind
Runs in front of car

Haiku – Flora & Fauna

Spindly leg spiders
Making great tangles of web
Invade Winter homes

Like coiled woolly springs
Fluffy new lambs leap in fields
Trying out young legs

Wordsworth's Spring heralds
Bright daffodils spill yellow
Like paint from tipped cans

Drifting on the breeze
Clouds of down umbrella seeds
Search for soil to grow

First green shoots through snow
Snowdrops grow flourish and bloom
Pure white heads bow down

Yellow aconite
Snowdrops' cheerful companion
Joins to welcome Spring

Dense caps of white flowers
Transform to shining black gems
Of elderberries

Round mistletoe ball
Beautiful parasite hangs
Green white berries bright

Lincoln Red cattle
Gentle creatures of the fields
Wear bright auburn coats

Fields of new green wheat
Wave gently in Summer breeze
Like ripples in sea

Hedgehog waddles slow
Shiny black nose spiney back
When scared a spiked ball

Huge flying grey clouds
Swarms of insects at twilight
Emerge just to bite

Of Seasons and Weather

Seasons and weather dictate much of how we live our lives

Cherry Tree

There are precious few landmarks to guide people along their way out in the farmlands, so we find that the cherry tree at the head of our driveway is extremely useful when guiding travellers to our home when they phone us lost, it can be seen from quite a distance, and a white painted house sign sits at its foot to confirm to our visitors that they have found the right address. Relatively small when we moved in, it has now reached its full potential height of around 30 feet, and while it bears no fruit edible for humans, the birds love it when its rich bounty of tiny wild cherries ripen. It is also a great barometer of the seasons, if you see a picture of our house, you can tell what time of year it was taken if the cherry tree is visible.

Cherry tree stands tall and proud
at the top of our drive,
Landmark for our home.
Our keeper of seasons.

Winter,
skeletal form of brown twigs.
Perfect lolly pop shape.
Tree sleeps,
no sign of life but the birds who flit in its branches.

Spring warmth revives.
Tight buds form,
split and spill blossom.
Clusters of white delicate flowers,
whose petals almost glow
when lit behind by early sun,
then later drift,
on Spring breezes,
sprinkle grass with soft snow.

Petals now shed,
Leaves bud and tree turns red.
infant foliage and tiny fruit
replace blossom.
Wild cherry jewels,
bright orange-red
attracting the birds
to feed on their riches.

Lawn now scattered with stones,
from cherries consumed.
Leaves grow bigger,
tree's green Summer clothes.
Each one saw edged,
they expand and unfold,
form lush canopy shading the road.

Autumn.
Air chills.
Leaves start to yellow.
Sharp frost over night
sets them alight,
red and orange bright.
Weary now, they hang tired, limp,
'til wind blows strong,
tired leaves lose their grip,
and drop
to lawn transformed to glowing red carpet.

Branches bare once again,
sap downward drains,
tree sleeps.
In hibernation,
awaiting Spring rejuvenation.

First Frost

While it is wonderful to wake to warm Summer mornings, sun streaming through windows in the early hours, I also delight in the frosty days of Winter. Still dark when I get out of bed, I watch the world transform from pitch black, to sugar-coated white as I make toast and tea and pack lunches. For a short while the world looks like a greetings card, clear blue sky, and a low sun picking out the glitter of frost, making everything sparkle.

Clear, full moon lit, night sky
lightens to blue,
pale and watery.
Edged dirty orange,
where lazy winter sun
struggles past the horizon.

Moon still haunts the Western sky.
Translucent, ghostly, globe
suspended in watercolour blue.
Pale reflection
of its warming companion.

Sun highlights white sparkle
on lawns and verges.
First frost of the year
dusts them gently with sugar,
like pies or pastries.

Temperature creeps up,
just over zero.
Frost on grass melts to sparkling dew.
Droplets endow
each green blade with diamond tip.
Brightly, in sun's spotlight, they glint.

Venture out.
Chill air nips
face and hands.
Dig gloves from pockets.
Thaw fingers.

Car windows, frozen opaque,
wait to be scraped.
Hoar, dislodged by busy scraper,
forms tiny white snow drifts,
perched on wipers.

On my journey,
watch strengthening sun melt lingering white
painting landscape with Autumn colour bright.

Sun's work complete before clock reads nine.
This was just a practice run
for real Winter yet to come.

Haiku – Winter and Frost

During my venture into the world of Haiku, I penned a few verses about the joys I find in Winter.

Shut out Winter's night

Gather round roaring log fire

Warm glowing orange

Cloudless frosty night

Stars shine bright like light behind

Pin-pricks in black card

Landscape edged with white

Glinting bright sugar sparkles

Of sharp Winter frost

Storm in a Teacup

We frequently holiday in Scotland, I'll not go into the complexities of the weather systems North of Hadrian's Wall, but just say that we've always been told that if the weather is not to our liking, wait five minutes, because it will change. We've seen a bright Summer day's temperature drop 10 degrees, skies cloud to black, and rain begin to fall hard enough to slow traffic, in the space of five minutes, and back again as quickly.

The Fen weather can do just the same, with no hills to stop a persistent weather front, you can watch clouds approach from the horizon, knowing full well that you will be getting soaked within minutes – quick, get the washing in!

Warm Summer day, bright sun, sky blue, but threat looms.
Humidity rises, and approaching from West, a vision of gloom.
Cloud-cover the colour of tea-stained paper,
dirty ochre creeps in, seeping into the atmosphere.

Gathering heavily, smothering light,
not too far behind it drags slate grey clouds.
Blown by the wind, suddenly gusting.
Approaching clouds spilling
grey smears of rain on fields not far distant.

Still bloated,
overloaded
with fat raindrops, they loom now,
overhead.

Murky ochre turns black, temperature's dropped,
sun's warmth blotted out, tentative fall the first drops
of precipitation.

Lightning rips, violent, through gathered oppression,
tears bloated clouds, spilling their contents.
Like grain from a split sack, fat raindrops fall,
splashing on concrete still Summer warm.

In seconds a few drips turn into a torrent,
as if clouds are soaked sponges someone wrung out.
Rain sets in, and a rumble of thunder shakes sky,
like the sound of huge bowling balls on an overhead alley.

Sound slower than light, it only just reached us,
before sky's lit once more by brilliant white flashes.

Sound, this time, comes quicker,
storm is much closer.
Rumble now crash,
once again blinding flash.
Now right overhead,
straightway thunder's heard.

Flashing, crashing crescendo, storm reaches its peak.
Rain starts to abate,
clouds roll on, wind gives chase

Storm shifts across landscape, we're left with last drops
from the edges of clouds, now rain's almost stopped.
Black clouds roll on over,
sky is now clear,
it's hard to believe storm was ever here.

Look to the East where the clouds have been chased,
still heavy with rain, fresh dry land they baste.
Roll on to perform storm's show in the distance,
until they disperse in the breeze at the coast.

Drawing a Veil

Every now and then we will open the curtains in the morning, and you could believe someone had frosted our windows, because you can't see any further than the window-sill. The clouds are so heavy they have extended from sky down to land, and lay thick over our damp fields and many waterways. Thick grey fog will sometimes hover around all day, hindering the drive to work. When you venture outside you walk into a mist of water droplets, getting wet as if it were raining, but no water falls, you are simply walking through low level cloud. The white misty variety, however, is vapour brought up by warm sun from damp land, rather than down from the sky, and can be quite beautiful. A low lying blanket of white cloud, like the mist that you see in photos of Scottish or Welsh valleys, it hangs particularly above the dykes and drains, obscuring the view down low, but the sky above it is clear. When the sun rises behind the white cover it makes it glow like a child's tented white sheet lit from behind by a torch, hope for the day, because sun will warm and evaporate the mist, drawing it upward to form a haze between horizon and sky, revealing the view.

Before I get to the main poem, I have included a haiku I wrote on the subject, during my "oriental period".

Mist rests low in dykes

Field borders shrouded in white

Like creeping dry ice

Fog, thick,
like a duvet across the land,
hides all from view,
low white cloud all around.

Away in the East,
Winter sun emerges from the horizon,
barely seen.
Weak illumination
through fog's heavy filter,
for a world slowly waking.

Rising higher,
it gains warmth
burning mist from behind.
A glowing white disc now,
higher still,
like a bright light bulb, round,
behind thick white curtains.

Fog surrenders to Winter sun's warmth,
revealing the landscape it had hidden from us.
First lawns, then driveway,
hedges and garage.
Grass verges, tarmac roadway,
the edges of dykes.
Mist clearing from drains
reveals hedgerows and fields,
as more melts away
we see houses and trees.

Sun's now beaten fog into full retreat
the distant horizon is finally revealed.
The world has awoken,
thrown off its bed covers,
we enjoy winter sunshine
and watery blue skies.

A Summer Afternoon

This poem holds a special place in my heart, it was my first "baby" after I began converting prose to rhyme. I sent it over to my dear cousin who had suggested that I write for a living, to see what she thought, keen to know if I had managed to "paint" the picture I had intended. It did get the seal of approval from the US, and was subsequently forwarded, I understand, to my cousin's friend who was terribly ill at the time and needed cheering up. I found the e-mail I sent to my cousin when searching for the original typed version of this verse. In it I had likened the act of converting prose to verse to that of placing photos in an album, making images make sense and tell a story. This story was inspired by our English seasons, which despite their erratic nature, I'd not be without, and while Summer in the farmland of Lincolnshire is relatively quiet, planting finished, harvest to come, the crops sitting quietly sunbathing and ripening in the (hopefully) Summer warmth, there is still plenty going on all around.

A broad sweep of sky, clear and bright blue.
A buzzard soars high, almost out of view.
Barely heard, he's so high, this magnificent bird
circling higher, in the air see him wheel.
Sharp eyes stare down, he scans the ground
on the hunt for his next meal.

A cotton wool cloud sits still, shining white,
in the brilliance of bright summer sun.
The air is so clear, making colours shine bright.
Green wheat toasts to gold as sun warms.

For a while a sound can barely be heard,
not a buzzing of insects, not the tweet of a bird.
They've hidden away, found a cool retreat
to withdraw to 'til twilight gives welcome respite,
then in hedgerows for supper they'll meet.

The sound of a mower strikes up in the distance,
a noisy reminder of man's existence.
And the happy squeal of children outside.
layered thickly with sunscreen, a mother's protection,
as they splash in cool water, run, swing and slide.

A clip clop of hooves on the hot tarmac,
passing ponies with riders on a summer's day hack.
Then the whir of bike tyres as cyclists glide by,
enjoying the ease of a flat Fenland ride

A dull hum from the sky, a small plane's passing by.
It's a flight just for pleasure,
to observe, and to treasure,
the patchwork landscape above which they fly.

The gentlest breeze stirs the cover of leaves
lush and green, it rustles the trees.
Close your eyes, in your ears the enveloping sound,
creates image of waves on sand, rolling shingle around.

The squeal of a hovering gull overhead,
drifted in from where river meets sea,
joins the rustle of leaves in the breeze to complete
the illusion of a day on the beach.

So I sit in the peace of this bright Summer day.
Lay back and relax, let my mind drift away.
Raise a glass to the silences and to the sounds,
to the breeze and the sunshine, and the life all around.

The Weather's Day Off

Anyone who knows me will tell you that I am obsessed with the weather. It's not so much knowing if we dare get the barbecue out, or whether I need sunscreen or an umbrella, it's more about the effect that weather conditions have on our landscape. The changing light from varying weather patterns is what brings much of our featureless surroundings to life, often to stunning effect.

The other thing people soon learn about me is that I have a strong aversion to words like "neutral", "easy listening" or "middle-of-the-road", phrases like these fill me with despair, I like bold, loud, vibrant. I like loud music, bright colours, exotic spices and gregarious, eccentric people. I like my senses to be excited and challenged.

Because weather conditions hold so much sway over how our surroundings appear, vibrant and exciting, or drab and dull, nothing makes my heart sink like a weatherman uttering the phrase "and the weather tomorrow is going to be mild".

The weather cannot be bothered today.
It's taken one look, and pulled up a duvet
of densely packed cloud, to cast the land
in a thick cloak of gloom,
drab grey all around

The weather's on strike, it just can't be asked
to do something wild, nor anything nice.

No sun to cast shadows,
no wind, not a breeze
to mess up our hair, or sway the trees

no heatwave, no snowfall,
no frost, sleet or hail.
No fog, mist or sunshine,
no downpours of rain.

Temperature sitting at 12 degrees,
too cold for tee-shirts,
but we don't need our woollies.

Weather's no strength to muster up gales,
nor icy blasts to freeze rivers and lakes.

No bright shows of lightning, nor thunderclaps loud,
it's the weather's day off,
so it will be "mild".

Turbulence

As previously mentioned, the Fens are notorious for being a particularly windy place, it's rarely truly calm, but the worst winds tend to strike in transitions between seasons, Summer to Autumn, and Winter to Spring, March is especially prone to blustery weather.

We wake to a blustery, windy morn,
roaring, turbulent gusts swirl and moan.
Bare branches on trees perform a wild dance,
long grasses bow down to worship wind's powers.

Sky thick with grey cloud, now torn by the gusts,
chasing the cover from West to coast.
Revealing in turn blue sky and the sun,
then white, and more grey, more clouds moving in.

It's like a playback of time-lapse photography,
the clouds fly so quickly across the sky.
Some stray Autumn leaves, still hiding in corners,
are whipped up in flurries, and flutter past windows.

Birds venturing out to search for their breakfast,
are blown roughly backward despite valiant efforts.
They flap energetically into the gusts,
thrown back in an arc, if for a second they stop.

Wind battered trees shed dry branches and twigs,
fragments are scattered 'cross the garden and drive.
The chairs and the table we sit at outdoors,
blown over, they're littered across the lawn.

With little to stop the wind's fierce advance,
it wreaks mischief and mayhem as it tears across fields.
In like a lion, out like a lamb,
it's the middle of March, dare we hope soon for calm?

Marching On

It's not just winds that March troubles us with, it is an erratic month when it comes to weather, we have often woken up to the unexpected. March 2022 treated us to weather which had us all packing away our boots and woollies, then in the last few days it decided to give us snow.

March won't go down without a fight,
open the curtains and over night,
what can I see laying all around?
a soft layer of white blanketing the ground.

Grass that had enjoyed basking in sun,
pokes tips above white to find there's now none.
A sky that was blue only yesterday,
is now cold and hard with clouds of steel grey.

The weather had teased us with twenty degrees,
but now the thermometer mercury plummets.
Though it is now Spring, March won't let us forget,
it can still flex its muscles, it's not over yet.

Our grandmothers told us that May must be out,
before we shed clothing, dare "cast a clout".
It could still snow in April, could still get us wet,
so don't shelve the sweaters or brollies just yet.

A Pictorial Interlude

While I sincerely hope that my poetry and prose is conjuring visions for you of our wonderful surroundings, I felt I also wanted to share a few of the photos I have taken over the years.

I have usually got my trusty Cannon digital to hand, because while nothing beats simply standing still and enjoying a moment, or a view, taking it all in, photographs are lovely to look back on later. A photo can set the wheels of memory in motion, and you can relive an event years on down the line. My photos have triggered memories for me of fleeting moments, never to be repeated, our ever-changing light and weather, plus sources of amusement and tiny wonders on our doorstep, inspiring me and helping me find the words to illustrate the captured moments in written form.

I have also included maps, to illustrate exactly where the Fens are. A modern map would have done the job, but I fell in love with the 17th Century one, with all it's old place names, and down in the bottom right a tiny corner of Norfolk.

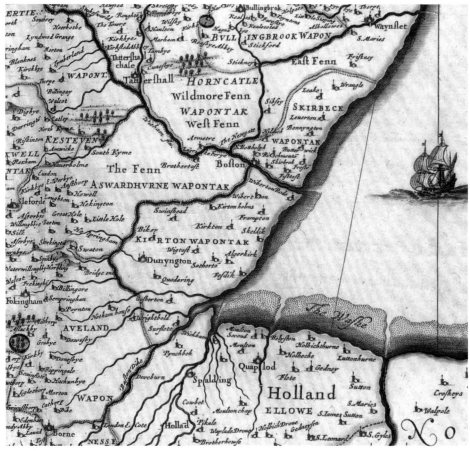

This map of Lincolnshire has been taken from Jan Janssonius atlas of England, published in 1646. This excerpt highlights The Fens.

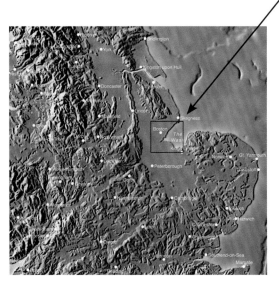

Our corner of the world

We live at the South-Eastern edge of the Lincolnshire Fens, just before Lincolnshire gives way to Norfolk.

Cherry tree marks
the seasons

Spring   Summer
Autumn   Winter

54

Summer colours,
like the dreams
Boy George
sings of in Karma
Chameleon - red
gold and green

Lush green lawn grass
bedecked with tiny cobwebs,
highlighted by morning dew.

Green velvet fields in December
develop to pure gold in August.
Harvest is a dawn to dusk job.

Vibrant Autumn colour gives way to Winter's chilly hues, with the ghost of last night's moon still in the Western sky.

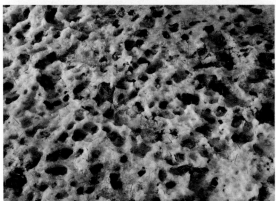

Brrrrr… We don't get huge amounts of snow, but just a sprinkling, or even a good heavy frost, sugar coats the landscape.

A thick, grey duvet of storm cloud rolls off toward the East coast after soaking the landscape.

Early morning Winter sun shines on water still standing on the paddock, and the dyke next to the house is as full as we've ever seen it.

Lighting effects. Precipitation, or just the threat of it, plays with light and colour

Soft Focus

Raindrops, moonlight and early
morning mist all blur life's edges.

Clouds can create wonderful illusions, there are no mountains near us, and this cottage has no wood fire. No illusions about the last one though, we were about to get very wet.

Both mornings and evenings can see the sky set on fire by rising or setting sun. Clouds catch the colours of the rays and create wonderful works of abstract art. These pictures are just as my camera captured them, no trickery.

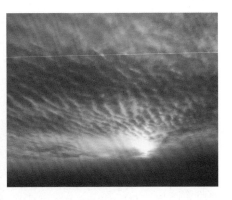

There may be just one view,
but it is never the same twice
thanks to the play of light
on the soft, ever-changing,
formations of cloud.

Raindrops and dew add sparkle to delicate beauty

Busy insects, a quirky double dandelion head bright coloured blooms, sparkling frost, or sprigs of rosemary gently catching a child's bubble, take a moment to appreciate some of the miniature miracles of nature.

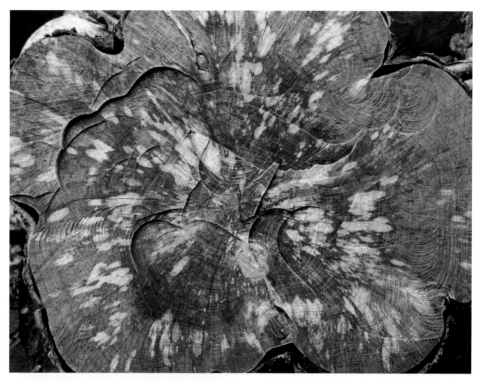

My Beautiful Log Pile.

Age, decay and the growth
of lichen have amazing effects
on the wood we stack to dry,
ready to be chopped into
smaller logs for burning.

We share our surroundings, and occasionally our house, with wildlife of many kinds, sometimes you see it, to the left one reckless rodent, and below Little Stinky and family, sometimes just the evidence of its existence.

I do hope you enjoyed the pictorial interlude. The front cover of this book is also a photo I took, like the rest, other than cropping to make it fit the space, it has not been altered in any way. The day it was taken rain threatened, the sky had turned a most peculiar sepia colour, and the altered light highlighted golds and greens in the foliage, very difficult to describe after the event, hence the reason my camera is never far away.

The one photo I did not take was the one of me, inside the back cover. I much prefer to be behind a viewfinder than in front of a camera, but my publisher insisted I should put in an appearance. So I enlisted a good friend, a keen and talented photographer, to take some flattering-as-possible shots for me. That was yet another day when anyone passing was probably convinced our house was inhabited by mad people. There was me standing on the edge of the road, clutching my camera and looking vaguely into the middle distance, our friend Steve with his camera, up a step ladder on the other side of the road to get a good angle (one without too many chins in evidence, though he is too polite to say that). Then there was Steve's wife in front of me trying to angle a light reflecting screen, clinging on to it to stop it flying off in the breeze, and my husband keeping an eye on traffic, making sure none of us got mowed down by cars or tractors. We don't get a lot of traffic, but there is no speed limit, and Sod's law decrees that if you only see one car in a day, that one car will appear when you are in the middle of the road. We managed not to get run over, but we did get some VERY strange looks. Thank you to our friends for spending a mad few hours with us, in the name of art.

Of Land and Sky

*The backdrop to our
lives, the flat Fenlands
and endless skies*

Cloud Art

Our endless skies, uninterrupted from horizon to infinity, provide the perfect stage for a particular form of performance art created by nature. Every day clouds provide an everchanging backdrop to our lives, as they drift and paint and scribble the sky with colour and texture, shading us from burning sun, providing us with rain, and warning us what the weather is sending our way next.

Sometimes bright baby blue, others pale aqua washes,
sky's a perfect blank canvas for cloud's artist brushes.
From a clear midnight blue, to a colour-drained evening,
or a thick heavy coat of drab grey emulsion.
Maybe soft whipped cream folds, white, no interruption,
each day a new backdrop, endless variation.

On far off horizon, is that cloud lying low?
Or rugged, tall mountain range, white-capped with snow?

Rising plumes of low mist against pale morning blue,
scribbling the sky with bright sunrise hues.
Doodles of mist, caught by sun's rose-pink light,
like they're written with neon highlighters bright.

Aeroplane vapour trails, ruler straight, white,
cut crisp, criss-cross lines across cold blue sky.
Then, like thin white paint on blue blotting paper,
they spread and disperse, finally disappear.

On bright summer blue, clouds create mackerel sky,
a beautiful lattice, pure, delicate white.
Formations of stripes, like those on the backs
of their silvery, glinting, marine namesakes.

Mares' tails gently curving, elegant wisps,
like the work of soft brushes, oriental techniques.

In a dark midnight sky, bright full-moon sits proud,
obscured and revealed in turns by cloud.
Moving art installation, up there in space,
wispy tendrils of cloud caress moon's lovely face.

Clouds, stained petal-pink by wakening sun,
splashed bright red and orange when at night it sinks down

Storm clouds paint a dramatic bleak picture.
Dark threatening black against dirty brown ochre.
They roll in from the distance, and drab colours seep
into white-pillow clouds they touch as they creep.
Then the turmoil of gunmetal colours above us
is torn and bright lit by lightning's forked flashes.

These beautiful works, on display short-time only,
pop-up exhibitions in sky's public gallery.
From white cartoon clouds, to grey heavy with snow,
each day guarantees a stunning new show.

Haiku – Clouds

*Such is my love of clouds, they just had to be praised in
haiku form too.*

Low bright orange sun

Paints clouds on the horizon

Pink welcomes morning

Sun sinks says goodnight

Sets fire to the horizon

Clouds glow vermillion

Fen View

This poem was inspired by a photograph taken by a friend of ours, one early Spring afternoon when we were out walking, near where the River Nene widens into mud flats and leaves the land to join the sea of The Wash. Despite the wide panoramic scope of the lens, the photograph of farmland shows little sign that humans were ever near.

Trees, stripped of leaves by Autumn and Winter,
identical like soldiers they stand to attention.
A regimental row of black skeletal figures,
patrol the field edge, shrinking to the horizon.

Stark fingers stretch, to pale winter blue sky,
playing host to small birds needing rest, passing by.
Tall trunks, strong and supple, to withstand the wind,
long roots reaching down, find safe anchor in ground.

Today air is still, no strong wind disturbs,
we hear every twitter, every songbird that stirs.
The field is a carpet of soft brown and green,
from rich soils emerge, bright green-shoot velveteen.

Gaze over the field that the tree soldiers guard,
the landscape rolls on, and with distance it blurs.
Colours of crops and soil, mingle and smudge,
at horizon, like watercolour, into blue sky above.

There's little to suggest that mankind exists,
except, trees and crops are in ruler straight rows.
And our high viewpoint, this grassy green bank,
is green coated by nature, but built by man's hand.

It separates salt marsh from rich reclaimed land,
stops the sea flooding our farms and our homes.
You see, without humans this land would be sea,
our flat Fens are nature, tamed by man's ingenuity.

Waterlogged

Our fields are generally very well drained because much of the area is sea level or below, and were it not for the efforts of mankind, transforming it into rich farmland, it would be marsh land. However, the ground beneath the fertile upper coating, is thick heavy clay, and this can be slow to drain when we get the monsoon-like rains we've had in recent years. Also, because there is no slope on the land, any slight depression will hold water like a huge puddle on an uneven footpath. While its mirror surface can give a dramatic interesting effect, this standing water can be costly to farmers if it drowns newly emerging crops.

Water on fields, standing, not drained,
surface still, like shining lake, mirrors sky bleak grey.
Puddles formed of rains, persistent, non-stop,
drop after heavy drop, on land already waterlogged.

Green shoots of cereal crops surround,
feet in soggy clay, they cling to life,
but under water's depths, others are drowned.

Wind blows, splits the clouds,
weak sun leaks through ragged tears.
Water's glinting surface ripples like sea.
Clouds blown clear, sky darkens, tonight it will freeze.

Smooth surface, now like ice rink frozen,
but no skaters are here to entertain.
Ice will thaw, land will drain.
Weather eventually warm again.

Shoots grow and ripen to golden ears,
but this year's crop will bear the scars
of water's ravages, Winter's frosts,
leaving the farmer to count the cost.

A Gap in the Clouds

I've always enjoyed my commute from home to work and back, the 20 minute or so break between work and home help separate the one from the other in my mind. Travelling early morning and late afternoon, depending on the time of year I could be treated to all kinds of fantastic light shows provided by rising or setting sun. On this occasion the low sun cut through cloud cover and appeared like a white-hot flame from a blowtorch cutting through a door from the other side, it briefly but dramatically highlighted colours and bright surfaces in the surroundings, then it was gone.

Oxyacetylene sun
slices through
the thick duvet of cloud settled on the horizon.

Light spills through the split
in the billowing white,
low, blinding, bright.

Sun white hot flame, light glows yellow and gold.
Bright fire highlights autumn leaves, glowing bold
in a darkening landscape.
Their colours shine vivid against gathering gloom
of approaching twilight.

Road signs yellow, red, and white
reflect sun's spotlight
and shimmer like jewels.

Hedgerows and bushes cast long shadows on fields.
Sprawling giants,
looming long, painting black
all in their path.

But this transformation of landscape is fleeting
Sun sinks low and clouds gather, sealing the tear.
Light fades, the shadows and colours disappear.
Sun sinks and our world descends into evening.

Harvest moon

I will never tire of seeing a harvest moon. The moon orbits so close to Earth that it appears huge on the horizon as it rises, and glows red with the sun's reflected light, it gives the impression of being so close you could almost touch it.

Of course, this event is not exclusive to the countryside, I must have seen harvest moons when I lived in town, but they didn't have the impact on me that they do now, because to witness their full glory you need an uninterrupted view of the horizon as the moon makes its initial glorious appearance, once above the level of buildings it begins to shrink with distance and fade.

Truly an unworldly sight
the Moon, in her rosy-pink harvest finery,
sailing close to our earth.

Emerges, huge, from the horizon,
like a gigantic hot air balloon,
glowing as the pilot applies flame to heat air.

A surreal apparition,
she silhouettes trees and hedges
as she floats up behind them.

She feels close,
you want to reach out and touch
this glowing Chinese lantern in the twilight sky.

Slowly she rises,
full and majestic,
above the stubble of newly harvested fields.

Rising ever higher on her night-time trajectory,
looking smaller now, with distance.
Pink party frock fading, light concentrating to bright white.
Party over, moon returns to her job of lighting the night.

Of Man
And
Farming

Not the most romantic of subjects, but both provide plenty of interest and entertainment.

Silver Giants

While nature provides much of the beauty in the countryside, some manmade structures have their own kind of drama and attraction too. Look beyond their intrusion into the natural landscape, and appreciate them in their own right, beauty is in the eye of the beholder, learn to behold fully before you judge.

My Mum was always fascinated by the giant steel pylons that stride across our country, carrying electricity to power our modern lifestyles, she always likened them to the brooms in Disney's Fantasia, Sorcerer's Apprentice, arms outstretched to carry their buckets, marching on relentlessly.

While perhaps individually ugly, these structures, with their miles of linking cables, carry your eye with them into the distance, as they shrink and disappear over the horizon. Sometimes drab grey, sometimes glinting silver in sun, these giants have been around a long time, and are as much a part of the landscape as barns and haystacks.

Great silver giants stride over our land,
insect arms outstretched, and from each hand,
a cable attaching each to its neighbour,
they stretch to the distance, man-made metal chain gang.

Like the magical brooms of Sorcerer's Apprentice,
they carry their loads across the landscape.
They bring us electric to power our homes
from squat grey power stations, and towering turbines.

Many see ugliness scarring the landscape,
but before you cast judgement, do double-take.
These creatures are there out of pure necessity,
but beauty is hidden in metal monstrosity.

When rising sun shines 'cross to western low cloud,
it paints pylons platinum against slate grey background.

At dusk, flocks of rooks, land on long curving wires.
They Caw loud goodnights, then to trees they retire.
Like black beads on a necklace, they gather and wait,
then, like a storm cloud, as one they take flight.

A sunset bright orange will silhouette, black,
The dramatic and angular towering shapes
of pylons, those close looming, like giants,
shrinking with distance, to straight rows of ants.

Thick fog covers land, the giants disappear,
'til slowly their misty cover starts to clear.
First one, then two, three, four more soon appear,
reminding us that the world is still out there.

Like abstract oil paintings, up close overrated,
stand back, hidden beauty can be appreciated.

Harnessing Nature

Most of the biggest landmarks in our area are man-made, and a great deal of them have been created for the purpose of generating and transporting power. We can see for miles from our windows, even from the kitchen downstairs we can see a cluster of wind turbines about eight miles to the East, and slightly to the right of them, the squat grey form of a twin-chimneyed power station. In a field to the South is a single turbine, only about a mile away, and from an upstairs window at night, we can see the winking red lights atop the chimneys of another power station some 12 miles North-West. The power stations could hardly be called attractive, but the turbines do have their own elegant beauty.

Elegant, tapering blades,
grey sails, turned slowly by breeze.
Air resists motion,
creates tangible noise.
Sound hardly there,
more felt than heard.
Whum … whum and swish
as blades slice the invisible
to create the useful.

Turbines drive generators,
cogs engage, turn,
power of nature creates power for man.
Lazy in motion,
like giant children's windmills,
punctuating the horizon.
Now highlighted, gleaming white
by low sun piercing clouds,
brilliant against storm-laden slate sky.
Now hidden by fog,
hanging low over fields
thick blanket conceals giants.

Some would say these monsters invade,
our unbroken landscape uninvited they raid.
But their balletic motion has rhythm and beauty,
their sweep and their swish perform vital duty,
important to all as our planet it bleeds,
from wounds we inflict meeting energy needs.

Haiku - Energy Production

Man's creations could not escape the Haiku bug either.

Lazy slow turning

Huge white blades swish through
the air

Turbines make power

Squat ugly building

Utilitarian grey

Belching out power

The Shoot

Not quite such a regular sight as they used to be, the shoot is still a part of country life, pheasant are mostly the prey of choice round us, the season being 30th September to 2nd February. Occasionally a brace of birds will be hung on our outside doorbell when the shoot has been on land nearby, though lately they are few and far between, with less shoots, and game becoming more "fashionable" lately thanks to TV chefs extolling the virtues of wild food, and teaching people how to deal with something that comes wrapped in feathers rather than plastic, they are more likely to be snapped up by anyone offered them, whereas in the past many shot for sport would go to waste.

There is a rhythm to an organised shoot, a convoy of 4 X 4 vehicles travelling round the back roads, stopping off here and there to bag a few birds, then moving on once prey in that field has been shot, or has fled.

First a shoot-inspired haiku verse, then my poem about the ritual of the shoot.

Loud pop of shotgun

In the distance pheasant drops

Dinner tomorrow

A convoy,
of farmers' 4 X 4 s,
takes over the farm tracks and droves.
Carrying tweeds and waxed jackets,
Range Rovers and Landies
pull up on verges.

Shotguns broken across their arms,
men spill into stubble fields and farmyards.

Load up,
take aim at the sky.
Beaters shout.
Pheasants fly.
Staccato sound.
Loud - POP! POP! POP!
Pheasants drop.

Prey, retrieved by soft mouthed spaniels,
is loaded onto clattering trailer
towed by ancient, green, Land Rover.

Tweeds regroup,
returning to off-road carriages.

From fields and verges
convoy reforms.
To the next shooting ground the party moves on.

Dinosaurs

There is an abundance of wildlife where we live, but the land is also inhabited by creatures not of nature. Agricultural machinery made horses redundant in farming when it appeared during the industrial revolution, though the primitive creatures of the Victorian age have evolved to huge technological wonders of modern times, which are almost making man redundant, never mind horses.

Like the workhorses before them, these creatures require attention and upkeep, but unlike horses, they do not need training, it's the farmers who purchase them who need to learn how to operate them. Shire horses working the fields is now just a romantic notion, a vision of the past, without their huge mechanical replacements, we could never meet the dietary requirements of our ever-growing population.

The more I watch these beasts toiling on the land, the more I am fascinated and impressed by what they are able to do. I have called them dinosaurs in reference to their size and power, certainly not because they are outdated.

Great dinosaurs roam out here in the Fens.
Huge jawed, heavy footed, they inhabit the land
Their colours are bright, red, yellow and green,
though blue ones and lime can often be seen.

The crawler it trundles, a great heavy beast.
It rumbles along on its Cat track feet.
They travel on roadways, and make the ground shake,
every picture knocked crooked as walls they vibrate,

A whine and a hum tell us what next will pass,
a gangly red sprayer with spidery arms.

Common as sheep in the fields are the tractors,
the real working horses of our agriculture.
Harnessed with tools from ploughs through to seed drills,
these versatile creatures have so many skills.

Late Summer's here and from hibernation
emerge the true giants of wheat cultivation.
Bright coloured combines come to eat up the crops,
hard workers from daybreak to nightfall non-stop.
With huge spreading jaws, their teeth spin and cut,
great bodies digest and process the crops.

They spit out the waste, it is left on the ground
for the scavenging balers to collect when they're round.
The balers collect straw and tie it up tightly,
in rolls and rectangles to stack away safely.
For animal bedding in cold Winter months,
the straw provides cattle with matting and warmth.

The bales they are huge, we need a weight-lifter,
the beast for the job - the great telehandler.
With a long sharp tusk, it moves in and impales
the hearts of the many enormous straw bales.
Lifting them bodily onto a trailer,
so the lorry can take them and store them for later.
This well-trained behemoth can also use arms
for lifting and shifting huge loads in farmyards.

The biggest of all is a green three-wheeled beast,
though a creature rare seen in the fields of the East.
Few roam the fenlands, their upkeep is dear
except in captivity, sightings are rare.
A majestic green dinosaur tall in the fields
powerful cat tracks round triangle of wheels.
Its rider must use a ladder to climb
to the saddle to ride this Fen farmers' dream.

There's so many species, way too many to name.
These beasts of the Fenlands by farmers are tamed.
We treasure the work of these powerful creatures,
as they help grow and harvest the crops that will feed us.

Big Dipper

As previously mentioned, the spider web network of dykes and drains criss-crossing our farmland are vitally important to the area, preventing the land flooding. For that reason, the drains must be maintained, which for the most part involves dredging them to prevent them being choked up by the abundance of reeds and waterweed which grows in the Spring and Summer. The greenery provides safe-haven for breeding waterfowl from Spring to Autumn, but once families have grown, and nests are no longer needed, man's work can begin. Long arms with spinning blades, attached to tractors, will reach down and mow grass on the steep banks, but the shallow water in the bottom of the drains needs dredging of debris. Flat bottom dredging boats work the rivers in the area, but the water in the drains is not even deep enough to float those. So, a land-based beast is employed, looking like a mobile crane, rather than a jib for lifting, it has a long arm with a wide metal basket attached, which reaches down from the banks and drags vegetation and debris from the water, ensuring that the drains are free-flowing and can cope with whatever precipitation Autumn and Winter send their way.

While these creatures rattle and creak in their labours, there is an elegance to their movement which can be quite hypnotic to watch.

It's Autumn, a creature appears in the landscape,
nothing of nature, this creature is manmade.
A heavy square body, and rolling Cat tracks,
an arching long arm to extend and retract.

It's to toil and to clear the abundant growth
of reeds with which waterways now are choked.
Its bright yellow body stands out in low sun,
six in the morning, work already begun.

Perched on drain banks, whatever the weather,
the long lazy dip and scoop of the dredger.
The elegant arm extends in the air,
a balletic sweep and its basket is lowered.

In water it lands, scoops foliage and mud,
then slowly retracts and the debris is dragged
by the giant metal basket, up onto the grass
and the dipper rolls on to make its next pass.

This mantis-like monster will slowly progress,
dipping and scooping, barely taking a rest,
'till drains are all cleared of Summer's lush growth,
and can do their real job of keeping us safe.

Safe from floods, as the Winter brings snow, sleet and rain,
water that runs from the fields and fills drains.
As it seeps from the fields, down through buried clay pipes,
he'll make sure there is room for it down in the dykes.

The Countryside's Haircut

Over the Spring and Summer, grass on verges and down drain banks is left to grow long and lush, providing cover and breeding places for wildlife and birds. However, once the wildlife leaves the exposed places, and hides away in the hedges and spinneys to shelter for Winter, the grass can have its yearly haircut. After harvest in late Summer, there are tractors free to begin the huge job of mowing verges and banks. Equipped with enormous cutting heads, or sometimes flails to trim hedges, they work from dawn to dusk, to complete the mammoth task before daybreak and nightfall pull too close together. For much of October you can find yourself stuck following tractors with mowing attachments as they make their steady way along the narrow roads, drivers skilfully manoeuvring machinery to avoid fences, road signs and telegraph poles. One such tractor is stored in the farmyard we live next to. Just before daybreak the driver arrives, parking his van, and taking the tractor out to begin work as soon as there is enough light to see what he's doing. In the evening we see the tractor lights sweep past our lounge window, the driver has worked until darkness prevents him doing any more, now he's leaving the tractor locked safe in the yard, and collecting his van to go home.

Harvest is over, the blonde cereal crops
are shaved down to stubble,
like they've had spiky buzz cuts.
Now that the fields have got their new hairdos,
the drain banks and verges
are waiting for theirs.

Tractors collect their hairdressing tools,
giant clippers attached,
they take to the roads.

They travel the countryside dawn to dusk,
eating through greenery
like giant locusts

Hedgerows are trimmed by a flail, spinning fast.
Not an elegant cut,
but one that will last.

They'll not need another, 'til next Summer's done,
birds finished nesting,
their youngsters all flown.

The verges are thick with Summer's lush growth.
Tall grass at road junctions
obstructing the view.

Tractors with mowers on long reaching arms,
trim the grass verges
and reach down the drains.

The mowers work busily clipping the grass
down to green velvet,
pass after pass.

Performing manoeuvres, they avoid clipping signposts,
like barbers with scissors
trim carefully round ears.

Soon it's all neat and tidy, to see out the year.
No growth now 'til Springtime
when new shoots appear.

The hairdressing tools all packed up at last,
the tractors return to more usual tasks.
The workhorses of the modern-day farm,
there's plenty to do, no long rest for them.

Of Nature

Nature can be entertaining, dramatic, and occasionally irritating.

A Talkative Lot

We do not hear many human voices where we live, having no near, human, neighbours, however there is no shortage of chatter from the neighbours we do have, from beast to bird, everyone has something to say. I'm not at all good at knowing which of our feathered friends sings which pretty song, but there are many distinctive voices out there that I can unmistakeably recognise. I know the chatter of a magpie, the cacophonous racket of rooks coming home to roost, and that if I hear "twit" and "twoo" from tawny owls there are two around, male makes one sound, female the other. I also know the sound made by a barn owl in flight, it is the single most unexpected, evil sounding, rattling hiss you could ever wish to hear. Don't believe me? Search the internet, listen to the recordings – your blood will run cold.

Everyone out here has something to say,
from the twitter of robins, to a donkey's harsh bray.
Competitive blackbirds "chip, chip" and chunter,
males issuing challenges, one to the other.

From the sheep in the fields, a throaty "baa, baa",
while a little lamb, lost, calls for his "maa".
The cows with their calves, peaceful souls on the whole,
will moo a loud chorus if they sense nearby meals.

Up in the ash tree, hysterical laughter.
The hilarious call of a bright green woodpecker.

Was that the squeak of a bike pump I heard?
No, it's the call of another bright bird.
With head glossy black, green wings, chest bright yellow,
the great tit's a fluttering, cheerful fellow.

A strange grating squark, sounds like faulty ignition,
but no car that won't start, it's a talkative pheasant.

Out ploughing the fields are tractors, pursued
by squealing white seagulls out scavenging food.
Opportunists flown in from the coast just to find
tasty fresh morsels in earth newly turned.

Wood pigeons cooing in Spring, all around,
are oft interrupted by much louder sounds.
They're a little too fond of tender new shoots,
to shoo them away, the bird scarer booms.

A magpie angrily chatters up high
in a tree, as the threat of a cat passes by.
Its relatives, crows, and colourful jays,
screech just as loud, always something to say.

A noisy black shadow of rooks come to roost,
calling their raucous goodnights in the trees.

At twilight the owl population converse,
each species possessing a singular voice.
The tawnies call out, one "twit" one "twoo",
oft heard, but always, hidden from view.

Despite lack of size, little owls can be heard
shrieking and squawking, such noise from small birds.

But there's one guaranteed to fill you with fear.
Silent in flight, the first sound you will hear
from the beautiful barn owl, when it's in flight,
is a spine-chilling hiss that haunts the night sky.

Clip - Clop - Repeat

The sound of iron on tarmac would probably not be the first thing to spring to mind if you were asked to name a relaxing sound. However, the gentle clip clop of the hooves of passing horses is just one of those sounds I would be happy to have in the background of life forever, likewise the roll of tide coming in on a shingle beach, or the gurgling of a stream over rocks. When I hear horses passing I always wish it was me enjoying the gentle bobbing motion of a trot along the road on a sunny afternoon.

Clip clop, clip clop, clip
A rhythmic gentle sound.
Horses' hooves,
iron shod,
clip clop on tarmac.
Walking slow,
calm, relaxed.

Riders,
hard hatted,
perched high.
Bobbing in time to the steady beat,
rise and fall of horse's broad back.
They speed to a trot,
beating quicker time as they pass.

Later soft thuds,
low rumble in the ground.
Hooves cantering
on thick grass
and soft mud on the bank.
A final sprint
on their way back.

Twilight Diners

From sound, to silent. We have never found out where our bats roost. But they are regular visitors at twilight, from Spring to Autumn. Just as the sun has sunk below the horizon, but darkness has not yet fallen, our swift-winged friends flit round filling their bellies with all the nasty biting, blood sucking, creatures that haunt the air in chaotic clouds at that time of night – Yay, Go bats !!!

Bats flit,

swift.

Black specks on twilight sky.

You step outside.

They dip and dive.

Wings whirr as they shoot by,

but never collide.

Pinpoint sonar

detecting insect dinner.

Circling the house

countless times.

Aerobatic show outside darkening windows.

They rush to feed

hungry mouths,

before darkness falls

and insects sleep.

I Hate Gnats

The title says it all. Despite copious amounts of repellent applied to exposed skin, if there is a flying biting thing around, it will bite me, I must taste good, as they will often choose me and ignore others. Insects breed in still water, and we are pretty much surrounded by still water where we live, sitting stagnating in the bottom of dykes. When we look out of the windows in the evenings, we can see swirling swarms of tiny insects, frantic as if all jostling for the same bit of space in the air. They are lurking, waiting for some unfortunate creature to pass by, so they can descend and steal a bloody meal. Gnats are one of the reasons I love to see bats around the place, they make a tasty meal for our tiny, winged mammals, the more the bats eat the less there are to make a meal of me.

Depending on where I am in the world, I could replace the word gnats with any given biting insect, midges in Scotland, mosquitoes in the USA, I've, unwillingly, provided meals for them all.

The form of this poem represents a swarm of my arch enemies on the attack. It's inspired by Lewis Caroll's "The Mouse's Tale" from Alice in Wonderland, one of my favourite childhood books, where the words of the poem are shaped into a long, tapering, representation of a mouse's tail.

I   hate   gnats
   twilight   flying
            over   water   swarming
                     spoiling   evening   walks
       gangly   legged   spindly
            winged
       work   of   the   Devil
    biting
         sucking
 creating   itchy   lumps
         red   wheals   on   skin
                     exposed   to
            vicious   insect   jaws
               they   land   and   stab

    sharp   pain   inflict
            steal   their   bloody   meal

        and   fly
            swollen   bellied   to   digest
                 and   fly   again
         to   stab   another
            unfortunate
                     victim

Space Invaders

In town we were used to a certain amount of wildlife around us, certainly garden birds, the odd hedgehog, urban fox. However our furred and feathered friends are a big part of our life out here "in the sticks". Most are more timid than their town counterparts, not so used to people being around, and don't need to come near us to find food, as there is a huge larder in the fields for them. However, this does not stop the odd creature thinking it might be fun to see where the humans live, and letting themselves in.

We have never got to the bottom of the crow behind the closed door of the dining room, it's like a Jonathan Creek mystery, how did he get there? And having disposed of the sooty remains of too many suicidal magpies and rooks, we finally got cages fitted to the chimney pots, so they can no longer fall in.

We don't always see people when we are at home
but visitors or no, we are rarely alone.
There's plenty of company here to be seen,
sometimes they'll even let themselves in.

For muntjac, our drive is a regular route
from the spinney and back when she ventures out.
Today she looks nervous, peers back over her shoulder,
as if she is checking for something behind her.
But it is not danger she looks for today,
it's her distracted and dawdling, tiny, brown baby.

In the stables a robin pops out from a box,
in a tool drawer she's built her tight-woven nest.
She got in through a hole in the door just to find
a nesting place, sheltered, all safe and sound.

The log pile is stacked at the side of the stable,
but when fetching logs we have to be careful.
Hidden there, sleeping, not emerging 'til twilight,
is hedgehog, a tightly curled ball of brown spikes.

A pair of house sparrows live up to their name,
when, in Spring, our utility loft they invade.
Behind the oil tank is a hole where they enter,
building their nest, raising family each year.

The occasional bird thinks it might be good,
to come in the house and take a quick look.
We once a huge crow in our dining room found,
opened the door, there he was, strutting round.
We think he got shut in the previous evening
it was hot, every window and door had been open.

Our utility once saw a sparrow hawk, flapping,
we had to employ a bath towel to catch him.
Then on hubby's finger he got a good grip
with strong raptor feet, his claws long and sharp.
Talons extracted, and avoiding beak's pinch,
we finally managed to get him released.
Briefly thought we had killed him, he laid and played dead,
but as soon as our backs were turned, swift, off he fled.

Sadly, not all the invaders survive.
Birds diving down chimneys are oft' doomed to die.
Searching for sites to build nests, they lean over
the chimney pot edge and fall in, don't recover.

So many creatures visit our house,
the rabbits, the pheasants, the occasional mouse.
The farm cats they come to hunt rats in the ditches.
The grey squirrels come to raid bird feeder's riches.

Such is the variety, between me and you,
I think we've enough to open a zoo.

Hungry Hoards

Whenever man turns soil to cultivate, birds move in to maximise on "fast food" dining. Man has done the hard work, dug up the insects and worms, now laying exposed on newly turned soil. Best spoils to the fastest, those who eat most are the ones who can get there before the squirming invertebrates have time to once more go into hiding. A robin or a blackbird will happily follow a keen gardener as they dig a vegetable plot, but on a larger scale, out in the fields, much bigger, and more competitive birds flock in to follow tractors with ploughs. Rooks and seagulls shout and squeal as they fly, sometimes you could believe that if you turn round you will see the sea, though we are ten miles or more inland. Rooks have always hunted inland, but seagulls have learned that it's worth a trip in from the coast when man is cultivating on a large scale.

There are seaside sounds, in the broad Fenland sky,
a flock of white seagulls wheel and cry.
Scavenging birds have flown inland,
to savour delights served up by man.

A scene straight from Hitchcock, they swarm round tractor,
as shining plough blades reveal tasty treasure.
Glinting white in the sun, they hover and twist,
jostling for space, rich spoils to the fastest.

By contrast, black rooks sit and patiently wait,
while tractor tempts seagulls further away.
As chaotic rabble, swoops, then moves on,
rooks patiently wait until they're alone.

A looming black shadow 'neath seagulls white cloud,
rooks settle in furrows gobbling morsels unfound.
Occasionally, edges of flocks touch and blur,
black and white dogfights break out in the air.

Their tactics the reason they can coexist,
seagull swooping and grabbing while rook quietly waits.
The contrasting methods of these diverse groups
ensure, on the whole, that everyone eats.

Heron

Even when we lived in town, we were not far from water. Our last house, and my parents' bungalow where I grew up, are within a stone's throw of rivers. There were fishponds at both places, which had to be netted over to thwart hungry, hunting herons from the riverbanks who'd often decide they'd like a change of diet from river fish, and try something more colourful in the form of goldfish.

We see herons most days now, they inhabit the banks of the drains, perched like grey spectres, often on the ends of wide concrete pipes that spill water drained from fields into our green banked flood defences, from where they get a good view of the still water below, and its edible contents.

Heron has competition for food these days. Until a few years ago the little egret was a rare species, however over the last five years or so their numbers seem to have increased dramatically. Now wherever we see herons, we also see their slightly smaller, pure white, fellow fishermen. The two appear to exist quite happily alongside each other.

Heron stands, neck outstretched, at the edge of the drain.
His feet in the water, he surveys his domain.
He's posed and alert for movement below.
Maybe a small fish in the water so shallow.

His neck muscles coiled and ready to spring,
his unwary prey will not know a thing.
A quick flash of movement so fast you may miss it,
the grey neck shoots out and heron has breakfast.
Unfortunate ducklings, sometimes a frog,
a newt or a tiddler all fall prey to the beak.

Appetite satisfied, Heron retreats
to his favourite daytime resting seat.
The grey wings unfurl, and he takes to the air,
his angular form like a winged dinosaur.

Modern-day pterodactyl with his lethal beak,
hunger now sated, peace and quiet he seeks.

Round concrete ends of giant drainpipes,
emerge from the banks, feeding water to dykes.
Heron chooses his favourite perch,
there to sit and digest 'til it's time for his lunch.

He lands and sits, shoulders shrugged, neck pulled back.
Ghostly grey apparition he haunts the green bank.

The Ballad of Little Stinky

Each year, for the last five or more, a pair of moorhens has raised a family in the dyke which runs close to our driveway. Most of the year we hear their strange, croaky voices, and the occasional splash as they enter or exit water, but we hardly see them. However, once the year's new brood are hatched, the sleek bodied black adults, with their white wing flashes and bright yellow beaks and feet, emerge to search our lawn for scraps left out for other birds, to supplement the diets of their growing youngsters. As the youngsters begin to grow, they will join Mum and Dad on their foraging missions, three or four miniature versions of their parents, but covered with thick brown down rather than sleek waterproof feathers. Their legs and feet are the same as their parents' too, long and thin, with the extended toes that wading birds have to prevent them sinking in mud. However, the youngsters are still getting used to their sprawling appendages, one can often be seen tripping another by stepping on a wayward toe or two, indeed they often trip themselves by stepping on their own, it takes time to learn to control feet as big as theirs. The family will only emerge when they think nobody is around, easily spooked by movement they will scuttle off, taking long strides, their heads bobbing back and forth in time with their legs, or necks extended, heads down and wings flapping for extra speed. This is the tale of what happened to one unfortunate youngster when I disturbed the family one day.

Stinky was a moorhen,
fluffy and brown,
a mere tiny baby,
still covered in down.

Huge clumsy feet, big enough to trip over,
by moving one foot, he'd step on the other.
He was searching for supper on the lawn with his siblings,
when I opened a door, and really upset things.

Mummy ran one way, Daddy another,
across to the left ran a sister and brother.
Just two remained, in a real state of panic,
shot off to the right, and under a pallet.

One youngster emerged on the opposite side,
of the other, no sign, he had disappeared.
My heart it plummeted down to my feet,
I feared I could work out the poor young one's fate.

Under the pallet lurked an old manhole lid,
weak and dangerous, totally rusted.
The lid was so rotten, all full of holes,
the pallet was placed there to prevent nasty falls.

Under the pallet, and lid - oh so rusty,
lurked a pit full of nasties, truly disgusting.
As I lifted the pallet, a faint squeak I heard,
confirming I'd found the unfortunate bird.

To the side the remains of the cover I throw,
and survey the sorrowful site down below.
A tiny brown shape, about three feet down,
on the contents of septic tank, paddling around.

Planning a rescue, I quickly procured
the spring rake to fish out the poor soggy bird.
I've done nicer things before I cook tea,
than fish in a septic tank, trying hard not to breathe.

I tried not to hurt him as I swept the rake round,
didn't want him to panic, and flounder and drown.
At last I manoeuvre the rake underneath,
the wriggling youngster and carefully lift.

A little brown bundle of fluff, all bedraggled,
now on dry land, to his feet he struggled.
Then off and away to find Mum and Dad,
I could only imagine they'd be so mad.

When he got to the dyke, all filthy and stinking,
Mum would chirp crossly "what on Earth where you thinking?"
"Off and away with you, stinky young thing"
"go swim around, don't come back 'til you're clean!"

Post script: Our septic tank was treated to a shiny new cover shortly after this incident

A Web of Deceit

Indoors, cobwebs are the bane of my life. Living out here in the countryside, every time the weather cools down, the house is invaded by arachnids searching for somewhere warmer to live. Consequently, I am frequently employing the clean sweeping brush that I keep specially for the task, removing their myriad dwellings from ceilings, corners and behind furniture. They are often built and attached so strongly I find a mere feather duster is simply not up to the job. The house can be cleared of these troublesome traps one day, then we find ourselves, the next, walking into an almost invisible thread strung across a doorway, or grabbing a handful of cobweb when we reach in a cupboard for something.

However, when outdoors, the architectural endeavours of our eight-legged companions can be seen in an entirely different light. They are miracles of biological engineering, and spiders' skill, beautiful, but lethal, works of art.

At first, they're invisible, tricking the eye,
may not notice these structures as you hurry by.
Almost transparent they hang in the air,
lighter than feathers, hardly know they are there.
Like finely spun sugar, long sticky threads,
from post to post strung and fastened each end.

Beautiful lace, forming deadly traps,
spiders' web nets hang in every gap.
Silk strong as steel to trap and ensnare,
unfortunate insects who dare to tread there.

Taut net will bounce like a trampoline,
alerting the spider it's time to dine.
Eight legs perform a delicate ballet,
crossing the net to attend to the fly.
No hope for this creature, first frozen by venom,
now tightly wrapped up, awaiting its doom.

Insects will see danger, but to our eyes there's beauty,
the garden's festooned when arachnids' been busy.
From door frames, trees and plants, trellis rungs,
on hedges and brickwork webs are hung.

Stretched stars of thread, pulled taut and strong,
embellished with spirals of silk, round and round.
Patterns like ripples in pebble splashed water,
concentric circles created by spider.
Lace work more delicate than any man makes,
spun works of art the spider creates.

When morning dew endows the silk
with sparkling jewels, by the thousand they wink,
in early sun they glitter and sparkle,
trembling as plants in the breeze they rustle.

At webs spun indoors we may mutter and curse,
as they hang from the light fittings, gathering dust.
But outside it's worth making sure that you pause,
admire the artwork of these beautiful snares.

Nature's Rainbow

I love a rainbow, who doesn't, we stand in awe when the sun shines through distant raindrops creating a full spectrum of colour which arcs across the sky, ethereal and magical, the stuff of fairy tales. But even without rainbows to enthral us, there is colour everywhere in the natural world, we must take time to appreciate it.

There's no need for rain for us to see rainbows,
Nature's own rainbow is everywhere round us.
We don't need to find a fine pot of gold,
just being outside is a fine reward.

Red is a fat harvest moon first risen,
and berries in winter yew, holly and hawthorn
The face of a goldfinch, a bright scarlet mask,
on woodpecker's head a vivid red cap.
Rowan tree branches bow low with the weight,
of vermillion berries on heavy seed heads.
Frost in the autumn causes green leaves to change
to red and bright orange, the colours of flames.

A sky fiery orange at night bodes good weather,
but a tangerine morn means you'll need your umbrella.
Robin's breast a bright orange, to impress the ladies,
rosehips, in winter sun, glowing with goodness.
Tortoiseshell butterfly orange wings flap,
Halloween pumpkins in fields growing fat.

First yellow of spring, aconites raise their heads,
bright daffodils follow, filling the beds
Hay fever inducing oilseed rape,
with luminous yellow it paints the landscape.
Gardeners curse fat dandelion heads,
and daisies' white frills round bright yellow hearts.
Great tits and blue flash buttercup chests,
and gold finches' wings sport bright golden flashes.

Green is the countryside's lush background hue,
sometimes almost yellow, others near blue.
From the grass on the verges, meadows and banks,
to the leaves of the trees on each twig and branch.
A lichen, a moss, a wildflower's leaves,
green rushes in dykes and lush waterweed.
Farm fields freshly planted sprout tender new shoots,
green shades by the dozen, producing our food.
Birds learn how to hide against this verdant colour,
from great tit's green wings to woodpecker's feathers.

Blue is the colour of sky in good weather,
pale aqua in winter, plumbago in summer.
Spot the blue tit's bright cap as he flies,
or blue eyes on the wings of peacock butterflies.
Another bright butterfly, soft powder hue,
the delicate, tiny, common blue.

The sky as the night takes a hold and sun sleeps,
turns a wonderful shade of indigo deep.
Blue plumes iridescent the magpie displays,
and Mallard drakes, indigo patches on wings.

Violet hues will oft tint the sky,
when sun rises or falls either end of the day.
Crocuses show purple heads early spring,
and shy purple violets on leaves emerald green.

My Beautiful Log Pile

As with colour, beauty can be found almost everywhere in nature, even in the most unexpected places. A large pile of logs inhabited one corner of our driveway for a long time, up until last year when my husband and his friend got round to splitting the large chunks down to fireplace size logs, to be loaded into our old stables for drying. Some of the pieces of tree trunk were over two feet across, and I watched the effects of age and weather on the surfaces of wood and bark, changing colours and textures, each day when I parked my car near the pile. A pile of wood took on a life of its own, and became a piece of installation art, the artist, Nature herself.

Log Pile, graveyard of trees long felled,
sad end to trees long life is beheld.

Brown carcasses, jointed like meat by a butcher,
branches and trunks, chopped and stacked in neat layers.
They await the attention of axes and saws,
to cut and to split, making logs for our fires,

Once magnificent trees, now's the end of their lifetime,
man's cut them down, as they're over-gown, rotten.
While awaiting its fate, the pile of dead brown
takes on a new life, and to beauty it's home.

For weeks and months it waits, sometimes years,
the heap transforms, new life appears.
Like grass and daffodils, blooming round gravestones,
dead wood is now gallery for new exhibitions.

Green bloom of lichen, once on branches too high
to see, can now be admired close by.
Still living in creases, and cracks of brown bark,
sea-green sculptural forms grow up.

Forming like delicate butterfly wings,
you'd think they were soft, like salad herb leaves.
But touch and they're solid, leathery, strong,
like fossilised, ancient, leafy fronds.

Alongside the lichens, fungi take hold.
Intricate structures emerge from the folds.
Where damp tree bark rots, the spores thrive and flourish,
embellishing logs with elaborate ruffles.
Frilled cuffs of pale cream, turning delicate grey,
as sun heats the log pile, and like wood they dry.

In a cut face of trunk, a life can be seen,
existence recorded in concentric rings.
Each year one was added, some wide, others narrow,
to those who can read, a story they show.
Of summers long gone, some wet, others dry,
a natural history of time gone by.

Like circular markings on vinyl, a record
of tree's long lifetime 'til finally felled.
Now weathered, the wood reveals colour and texture,
cream yellow turns grey, and cracks start to rupture
the surface of wood as it dries in the sun
the transformation to fuel has begun.

But this is not the end of the story,
changes in colour reveal more hidden beauty.
A broad ring of growth, a patch of dark rot,
the incision of chainsaws, the curl of a knot.
What once was bland surface of newly felled wood,
is now ever-changing, natural art.

Light Relief

There are so many things in life that we have to take seriously, and things we see every day, on TV or in the papers, that are distressing and upsetting, we must find levity where we can, or we will all go mad. So my last two poems for this volume are of a light hearted nature, we all need a bit of "lol".

Complacency Kills

The only thing pheasants are good for is the pot. Day to day they are a nightmare. The average pheasant has no road sense, strutting along nonchalantly as cars speed toward them. There are acres of fields they could strut happily, and safely around in, but they choose the tarmac. And when it comes to escaping danger, despite having wings to fly with, they choose to run up the road in front of you, trying to outrun impending doom. On the odd occasion they do decide to take off when a vehicle startles them, they seem to head across the road in front of it, rather than into the verge. It would not matter so much were they a tiny bird, but a couple of pounds of pheasant can do an amazing amount of damage to bodywork, front grilles or headlights. Sometimes I think as many pheasants are killed by vehicles as shotguns.

Pheasant feels safe, he struts along smugly,

"Game season's over, I know you can't shoot me".

But pheasant beware, do not be so complacent,

you strut on the road, and here comes a boy racer.

Reckless Rodent

Grey squirrels abound in the spinney next to our house, they are very cute to look at, and impressive acrobats, skipping through the trees and sitting up high, nibbling on tasty morsels clasped between tiny grey paws. However, they are also destructive thugs, who will stop at nothing to get those tasty morsels, and like nothing better than the contents of bird feeders, seed and peanuts. We have finally managed to find some feeders from which they cannot extract the contents, and put the bird table up high, away from anything they can jump off to get to it, and it has a metal skirt halfway up its pole to prevent them climbing. It took years to thwart the furry grey things, and cost a good deal in feeders that either failed to be "squirrel proof" as advertised, or were nibbled through and destroyed by the pesky critters. One of the peanut feeders we bought was of the kind you see a lot for sale in garden centres, it had a long round cage for the peanuts, with a larger cage round it that birds could get through, but not squirrels, well that was the theory. My son looked out of the kitchen window one day to see a panic-stricken squirrel wedged firmly between the outer cage, and the inner peanut cage, which he had chewed a hole in to extract his meal, but had then found that getting out of the cage was not quite as easy as getting in. After taking a few amusing photos of the unfortunate creature, my son risked life and fingers extracting the ungrateful biting, scratching rodent. I felt that a limerick was fitting for such a comic tale.

A silly young squirrel got stuck

in a cage when he tried to steal nuts.

His struggles impotent,

the unfortunate rodent

had to wait from the cage to be plucked.

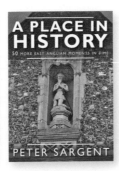
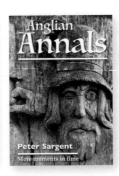
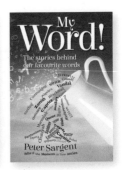

PAUL DICKSON BOOKS
Books by Norfolk writers published in Norwich

Paul Dickson has lived and worked in Norfolk for the past 33 years, initially for the National Trust, then as an independent PR practitioner and latterly as an independent publisher and tour guide.

A meeting with Illuminée Nganemariya in 2006 saw Paul assisting with Miracle in Kigali, Illuminée's story of survival during the Genocide against the Tutsis in Rwanda and subsequent life in Norwich.

After a spell as a director of Norfolk's Tagman Press, Paul decided to branch out on his own in 2016. Since then he has embarked on collaborations with Norfolk writers, Tony Ashman, Janet Collingsworth, Sandra Derry, Steven Foyster, Neil Haverson and Peter Sargent.

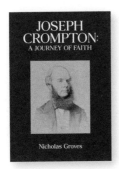

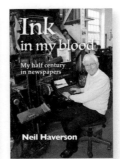
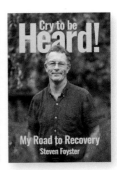

www.pauldicksonbooks.co.uk